CELEBRATE!

CONNECTIONS AMONG CULTURES

BY JAN REYNOLDS

LEE & LOW BOOKS INC. • NEW YORK

To Jennifer Fox and her big celebration, May 8, 2004—J.R.

Pronunciation Guide

Many of the foreign words in this book have been adapted into English from the societies' native languages. Some variations in spelling and pronunciation may exist.

Aborigine (ab-eh-RIJ-eh-nee)
Balinese (bah-li-NEEZ)
Dar Moulay (DAR moo-LAY)
didgeridoo (DI-jeh-ree-dew)
dzi (dzee)
gamelan (GAM-ah-lon)
heris (HARE-eez)
Himalaya (him-mah-LAY-uh)
Inuit (IN-yu-it *or* I-nu-wet)
Kayavak (KI-yah-vak)

Kaylauzak (KI-lao-zak)
lamas (LA-mahz)
lavu (LA-voo)
Legong (LAY-gong)
mandalas (MAN-de-leh)
Mani Rimdu (MA-nee RIM-dew)
onoto (oh-NO-toe)
Sami (SAH-me)
Sanghyang (SONG-young)
shaman (SHAH-men)

shaponos (shaw-POE-noze)
Sherpa (SHER-pah)
sinew (sin-YOU *or* sin-EW)
Thami (TAH-me)
Tibetan (te-BEH-ten)
Tuareg (TWAH-reg)
ululating (ULL-you-late-ing *or* YOOL-you-late-ing)
Yanomami (ya-noh-MA-meh)
zendi (ZEN-dee)

ACKNOWLEDGMENTS

Special thanks to researcher Michelle Harris for additional help in confirming cultural information—J.R.

Photograph of family celebrating Thanksgiving on page eleven copyright © Larry Williams/CORBIS

Manufactured in China by Jade Productions, January 2010
Book design by Tania Garcia
Book production by The Kids at Our House
The text is set in Futura Book
(HC) 10 9 8 7 6 5 4
(PB) 10 9 8 7 6 5 4 3 2 1
First Edition

Library of Congress Cataloging-in-Publication Data
Reynolds, Jan.
  Celebrate! : connections among cultures / by Jan Reynolds.— 1st ed.
    p. cm.
  Summary: "Photo-essay that explores the similarities among celebration rituals in several indigenous cultures around the world and compares them with celebrations in the United States. Includes a map and an author's note"—Provided by publisher.
  ISBN 978-1-58430-253-7 (HC)   ISBN 978-1-60060-452-2 (PB)
1. Holidays—Juvenile literature. 2. Festivals—Juvenile literature. 3. Fasts and feasts—Juvenile literature. I. Title.
GT3933R49 2006
394.26—dc22   2005015312

I had the wonderful opportunity of celebrating with all the people you will see in my photographs. Some of their communities are nestled in remote corners of the world, and their cultures are among the oldest still in existence.

I lived with these families, sharing their homes, food, and daily lives. I joined in their special festivities and ceremonies. The celebrations were big and small, lasting several days or just a few minutes. They marked changes in people's lives, expressed thankfulness, and honored important people and events.

On the surface these celebrations may appear to be different from one another, but observing them firsthand I realized all of these societies were really doing the same things to celebrate; they were just doing them in their own ways. I also discovered that these ceremonies and festivities based in ancient cultures have a lot in common with our modern celebrations.

Experiencing these connections among celebrations showed me it doesn't matter which language we sing in or what color our skin is underneath our costumes or clothing. We are much more alike than we are different. So let's celebrate together, as one human family!

Jan Reynolds

Jan Reynolds and her husband at their wedding, a Sherpa *zendi* celebration, in the Everest region of the Himalaya.

WHEN WE CELEBRATE . . .

Tibetans and Sherpas of the Everest region of the Himalaya gather in the Thami Valley for *Mani Rimdu*. For three days during the celebration, people receive blessings for good health and good fortune from spiritual leaders called *lamas*.

WE GATHER TOGETHER

In the spring, Sami gather to celebrate the return of sunlight to the Arctic region of Northern Europe. The days are much warmer and longer, and people meet up with family and friends they have not seen all winter.

Hundreds of Tuareg come together in the center of the Sahara desert to celebrate *Dar Moulay.* They gather every spring for this three-day celebration, starting on the eve of a full moon. The festivities honor the life of Moulay, an ancestral hero known as a great leader and healer of the sick.

A Yanomami community in the Amazon gathers because someone in the village has died. Close relatives and friends parade around the village to say good-bye and wish the person well in the spirit world. Together they celebrate the life they shared with their friend and loved one.

Inside an igloo, Inuit in the Arctic come together to sing *Kayavak*. One person makes a unique throaty sound into a large pot, which amplifies the sound. A second person in turn tries to imitate the sound of the first. This goes back and forth faster and faster, until one of the singers makes a mistake and they break into laughter.

On the South Asian island of Bali, one hundred men traditionally gather for the chorus of an ancient dance ritual called *Sanghyang*. The men chant softly, over and over, their voices uniting in a rhythmic melody to accompany dancers. This ancient celebration connects the Balinese with their ancestors.

Americans get together on the fourth of July to celebrate Independence Day and the birth of the United States as a nation in 1776. The fourth of July is traditionally marked by parades with local citizens, fire trucks, and floats; picnics and barbecues; and nighttime displays of colorful fireworks.

WHEN WE CELEBRATE...

These Tuareg men drink tea to celebrate the upcoming marriage of a relative. As they share their drink, anyone who objects to the marriage has a chance to speak. The tea is made with strong mint and lots of sugar, which coats and soothes parched, dry throats.

WE EAT AND DRINK

This Inuit family eats slices of frozen raw fish to give thanks for their good catch. The Inuit fish through holes cut in the thick ice covering lakes. Some still use traditional fishing methods: lines of sinew wound on sticks, hand-carved hooks made of animal bones, and caribou flesh for bait.

The Balinese bake elaborate cakes for celebrations. This cake is for a wedding and represents the entire universe. The pictures at the bottom show the lower world where evil lives. The man and woman in the middle represent life on Earth. Everything above the couple represents goodness in the heavens.

An Aboriginal boy catches a carpet snake curled inside a hollow log. The snake will be roasted and eaten to celebrate *walking on a Dream Journey.* When walking on a Dream Journey, Aborigines travel ancient pathways they believe were originally traveled by their ancestors. This reconnects them with their land and spiritual past.

A Yanomami man carries two armadillos that have been roasted over an open fire. Armadillo is a special food for the Yanomami and is only served on important occasions. Today the armadillo will be eaten to honor a member of the community who died.

Sami reindeer herders celebrate the return of spring with a big batch of reindeer stew. During winter in the far north, it is dark most of the day and night, and the Sami depend almost entirely on reindeer for food. When the sun returns in spring, the Sami add berries and fish to their meals. The reindeer stew symbolizes the end of their winter diet.

A family in the United States gathers for a turkey dinner to celebrate Thanksgiving. The tradition commemorates a time in North American history when Native Americans helped early settlers learn to live off of the land. At harvesttime, they all shared a feast of wild game and crops they had grown. Today Americans gather with friends and family to give thanks for the good things in their lives.

These Yanomami women decorate their faces for a celebration using paste made from onoto seeds. To make the paste, the women pull sticky red onoto seeds from pods and crush the seeds with their fingers. Black paste is created by mixing ashes into the crushed red seeds. The sticks in the women's faces are worn daily.

WE DECORATE OURSELVES

For special occasions, Aborigines decorate themselves with paint made from natural materials that they gather, such as rocks and roots. These materials are baked, pounded into powder, and mixed with water to make paint in shades of red, brown, and yellow.

A young Tuareg boy dips a wet stick into a pouch filled with ashes. Using the stick, he decorates his eyes, darkening his eyelids and eyebrows. Like other Tuareg males, when he wears his indigo-colored veil for Dar Moulay, only his decorated eyes show.

An Inuit boy is dressed up as a wolf, wearing a real wolf skin. His family is celebrating a good hunt. The boy's father hunted the wolf after it attacked the family's caribou herd. The boy's mother prepared the wolf skin to preserve it and may later trade it at the fur market.

This Sami girl wears traditional clothes for the spring festival celebration. Her curved-toe shoes are made from reindeer hide and sewn with thread made of reindeer sinew. The festival includes reindeer roping contests, sleigh rides, and reindeer races.

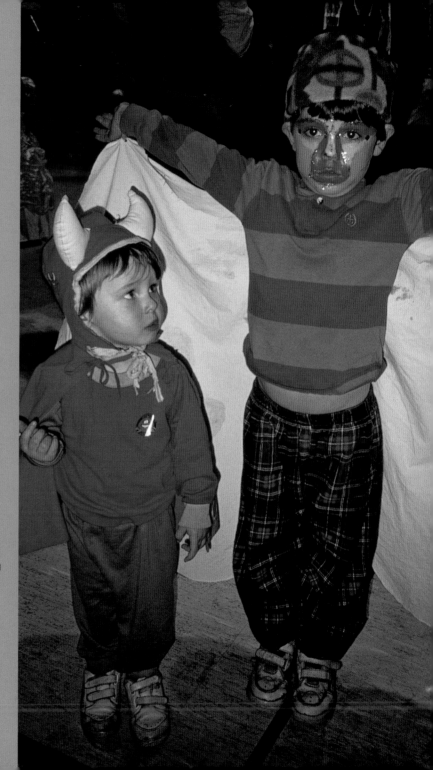

This woman in Tibet is decorated with special beads for a *zendi*, a wedding celebration. The beads are made from turquoise (greenish beads), coral (red beads), and amber (the yellow bead). One of the rarest and most highly-valued beads is the black-and-white *dzi* bead, such as the ones in this woman's hair.

Children in the United States wear costumes for Halloween. The celebration of Halloween evolved from Celtic traditions marking the transition from summer to the darker days of winter. During this time of year it was thought spirits could communicate with the living. People wore costumes to ward off any evil spirits.

WHEN WE CELEBRATE...

The Inuit perform *Kaylauzak*, a meditative drumming and dancing, to celebrate a successful caribou hunt. The Inuit honor the caribou by using all parts of the animal.

Bones are used for tools; sinew for lashing and thread; meat for food; and skins for clothing, bedding, and musical instruments.

WE PLAY MUSIC

When a Sami *shaman* beats his reindeer hide drum, he is celebrating his connection with the natural world. It is believed the shaman has special abilities to communicate with the spirits of nature. Because of this, people in his community ask him questions such as "How long will the winter continue?" and "When will the good rains come?"

This Aboriginal man plays the *didgeridoo*, an instrument made from a eucalyptus tree branch that has been hollowed out by termites. Part of many Aborigine celebrations, didgeridoos are very difficult to play. The musicians make continual music using circular breathing—breathing in through the nose while blowing out through the mouth.

At the celebration of Dar Moulay, Tuareg men beat their drums in a complicated musical rhythm. Several different beats may be heard at the same time. Women join in by *ululating*—making loud, high-pitched sounds in their throats while rapidly moving their tongues from the front to the back of their mouths.

Tibetan musicians blow large, ancient seashells to call for blessings of good fortune throughout the year. The deep sounds from the shells can be heard for miles, bringing comfort to all who hear them. These shells are still found in the high Himalaya, indicating that long ago this area was under the sea.

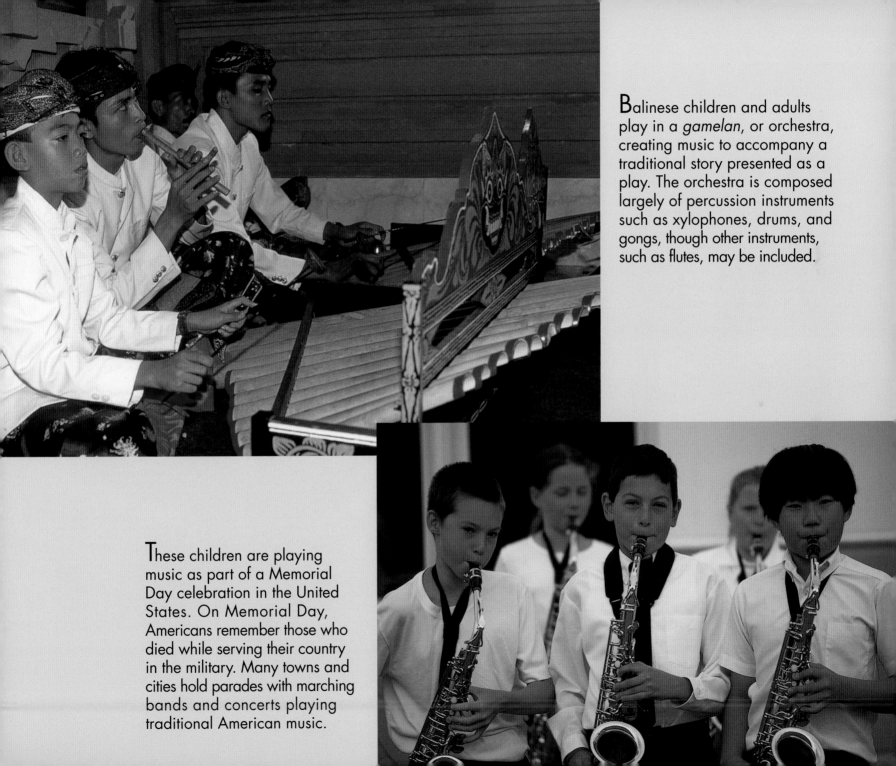

Balinese children and adults play in a *gamelan*, or orchestra, creating music to accompany a traditional story presented as a play. The orchestra is composed largely of percussion instruments such as xylophones, drums, and gongs, though other instruments, such as flutes, may be included.

These children are playing music as part of a Memorial Day celebration in the United States. On Memorial Day, Americans remember those who died while serving their country in the military. Many towns and cities hold parades with marching bands and concerts playing traditional American music.

WHEN WE CELEBRATE....

The *Legong* dance, performed by these women, celebrates a traditional story that is an important part of Balinese history. The story illustrates the value of love and truth, as a prince fights to win back his princess. Accompanied by the quick tempo of the gamelan, many of the dancers' movements are precise motions of the eyes and fingers.

WE DANCE

Yanomami dance as they sing *heris*, songs of thanks for good fortune, such as a bountiful hunt. Heris are sung at dusk every evening when Yanomami of all ages gather together in open areas within their large *shaponos*—thatched grass huts that house up to one hundred extended family members.

In the ceremonies of Mani Rimdu, dances tell old stories about how to live a loving, compassionate life. Traditionally only monks read the ancient texts, so they danced and acted out the stories for the community. Many dances are humorous, allowing the audience to laugh while learning a lesson from the story.

When they are born, Aboriginal children are given animal names along with their family names. The animal names are called their *dreaming*. The Aborigines believe that when they *dance their dreaming*—pounding the earth with their feet—they reconnect with the time of creation and the creators of all life.

Dancing is a common part of many Tuareg celebrations. The rhythm of a drum compels men to move to the beat and join in the dancing during this casual gathering. The dance is individual, and all are welcome to stand and express themselves.

Every summer in the United States, the Bread & Puppet Theater of Vermont uses dances and puppets to act out stories celebrating life. During the festivities, the theater group also serves bread to everyone gathered. The sharing of bread symbolizes the connections of community, while the dances celebrate human creativity and self-expression.

WHEN WE CELEBRATE...

This Sami family lights a fire inside their *lavu*, a structure traditionally made of tree saplings covered with reindeer skin. Spring is here and it is time for the reindeer roundup, when calves are lassoed and brought in for marking. Through the night, as reindeer are tallied, stories are told around the fire.

WE USE FIRE

An Aboriginal man creates a smoky fire at a celebration to send off the spirit of a relative who has recently died. He believes his thoughts will rise with the smoke and urge his relative to leave Earth and life in human form. This is the time for the relative's spirit to travel to the spirit world.

A *mandala*, an ornate painting often made from naturally dyed river sand, is being burned in a Tibetan celebration. Burning the mandala symbolizes the idea that human beings should let go of material objects not essential to life. After the mandala is burned, the sand is returned to the river, which represents the flow of life.

Balinese men chant at a celebration in which a young man rides a "horse" made from dried grass over burning coconut shells. The young man's feet land on the hot coals as he moves back and forth. By fire walking the young man demonstrates that he has achieved a deep, trancelike level of relaxation and inner calm.

Fire is an essential part of Tuareg celebrations. At this wedding, men and women build separate fires. The fires are used for cooking bread and pots of camel meat, and are also a gathering place for passing on knowledge from man to man and woman to woman.

When Americans celebrate their birthdays each year, they put lighted candles on their birthday cakes. It is believed that this practice started with the ancient Greeks. Traditionally, the birthday celebrant makes a wish and tries to blow out all the candles at once. If he or she succeeds, the wish will come true.

THERE ARE MANY WAYS TO CELEBRATE THE HUMAN SPIRIT

Although cultural celebrations around the world may not look the same, they actually have a lot in common. We all celebrate things for which we are thankful, changes in our lives, and important people and events. We all eat and drink, decorate ourselves, sing and dance, and use fire. We all gather together with family, friends, and neighbors to share these special times in our lives.

We are one human family celebrating life on Earth!

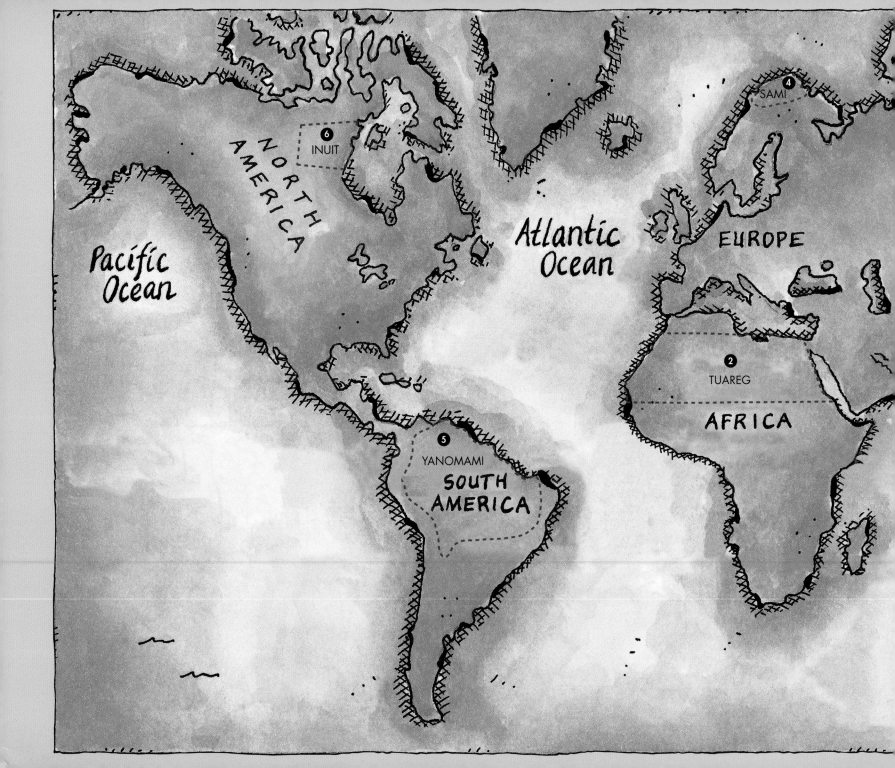

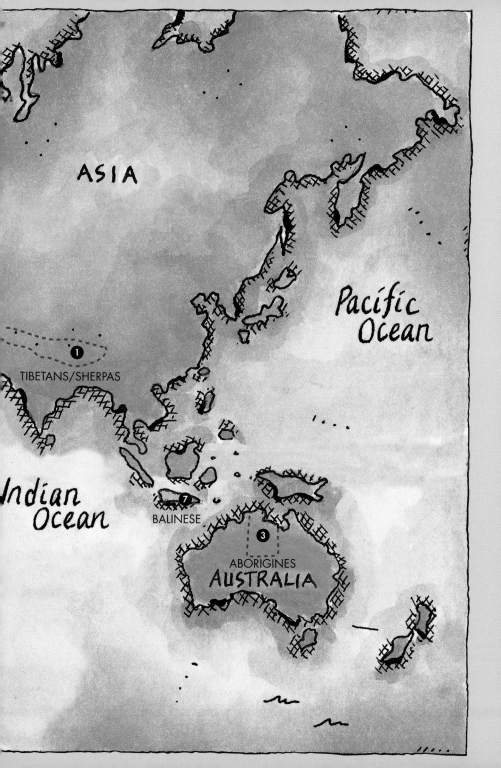

ASIA

Pacific
Ocean

Indian
Ocean

TIBETANS/SHERPAS

BALINESE

ABORIGINES
AUSTRALIA

1 Tibetans and Sherpas live in the Himalaya, the highest mountains on Earth, which include Mount Everest.

2 The Tuareg, nomads who traditionally travel by camel caravan, live in the Sahara, the largest desert in the world.

3 The Aborigines of Australia live in the rugged outback, hunting along the ancient paths of their ancestors.

4 The Sami live on the northern tip of Europe in a land area that falls mostly within the Arctic Circle.

5 The Yanomami live in the Amazon basin of South America, home to the largest rain forest in the world.

6 The Inuit, whose traditional way of life relies on caribou, live in the far north of the North American continent.

7 The Balinese, a rice-farming people, live on one of the tropical islands of Indonesia in South Asia.

Sources
Much of the research for this book came from the author's field work and primary observations while living with the indigenous cultures presented in the text.

Additional Sources
ALL CULTURES
Bowker, John. *World Religions*. New York: DK Publishing, 1997.

Campbell, Joseph, ed. *Myths, Dreams, and Religion*. New York: E. P. Dutton, 1988.

National Geographic Society, ed. *Vanishing People's of the Earth*. Washington DC: National Geographic Society, 1968.

Smith, Huston. *The Religions of Man*. New York: HarperCollins, 1986.

Steichen, Edward. *The Family of Man*. With prologue by Carl Sandburg. New York: Simon and Schuster, 1988.

Swartz, Marc J., and David K. Jordan. *Culture: The Anthropological Perspective*. New York: John Wiley and Sons, 1980.

ABORIGINE (AUSTRALIA)
Chatwin, Bruce. *The Songlines*. New York: Viking/Penguin, 1987.

Cowan, James. *Mysteries of the Dreaming: The Spiritual Life of the Aborigines*. Bridport (Dorset), UK: Prism Press, 1989.

Isaacs, Jennifer. *Australia Dreaming: 40,000 Years of Aborigine History*. Melbourne, Australia: Landsdowne Press, 1981.

Lawlor, Robert. *Voices of the First Day: Awakening in the Aborigine Dreamtime*. Rochester, VT: Inner Traditions, 1981.

Neidjie, Bill, Allan Fox, and Stephen Davis. *Australia's Kakadu Man Bill Neidjie*. Darwin, Australia: Resource Managers, 1986.

Sutton, Peter. *Dreamings: The Art of the Aborigines in Australia*. New York: George Braziler Publishers with Asia Society Galleries, 1988.

BALINESE (SOUTH ASIA)
Eiseman, Fred B., Jr. *Bali: Sekala and Niskala: Essays on Religion, Ritual, and Art*. Hong Kong: Periplus Editions, 1990.

Greenway, Paul, James Lyon, and Tony Wheeler. *Bali and Lombok: Island Dharma and Kuta Karma*. Oakland: Lonely Planet, 1999.

Lansing, J. Stephen. *Priests and Programmers*. Princeton, NJ: Princeton University Press, 1991.

INUIT AND SAMI (ARCTIC)
Annaqtuusi, Ruth, and David F. Pelly. *Qikkaaluktut: Images of Inuit Life*. Oxford, UK: Oxford University Press, 1986.

Brody, Hugh. *Living Arctic: Hunters of the Canadian North*. Seattle: University of Washington Press, 1987.

de Poncins, Gontran. *Kabloona: Among the Inuit*. New York: Carroll and Graf, 1988. First published 1941 by William Morrow.

Farley, Mowat. *The Desperate People*. Toronto: Seal Books, 1980. First published 1959 by McClelland and Stewart.

Freuchen, Peter. *Book of the Eskimos*. Cleveland: World Publishing Co., 1961.

Gaup, Ailo. *Trommereisen*. Oslo, Norway: Gyldendal, 1988.

Harner, Michael. *The Way of the Shaman*. New York: Bantam, 1986. First published 1980 by Harper and Row.

Lopez, Barry. *Arctic Dreams*. New York: Charles Scribner's Sons, 1986. Bantam Reprint, 1989.

TIBETAN/SHERPA (HIMALAYA)
Dalai Lama. *The World of Tibetan Buddhism*. Boston: Wisdom Publications, 1995.

Fantin, Mario. *Mani Rimdu Nepal: The Buddhist Dance Drama of Tenpoche*. Singapore: Toppan Co., 1976.

Furer-Haimendorf, Christoph von. *Himalayan Traders*. London: John Murray Publishers, 1975.

Thurman, Robert A. F. *Inside Tibetan Buddhism: Rituals and Symbols Revealed*. San Francisco: Collins Publishers, 1995.

TUAREG (SAHARA)
Fisher, Angela. *Africa Adorned*. New York: Harry N. Abrams, 1984.

Porch, Douglas. *Conquest of the Sahara*. New York: Fromm International Publishing Corporation, 1986.

YANOMAMI (AMAZON)
Chagnon, Napoleon A. *Yanomamo: The Last Days of Eden*. New York: Harcourt Brace Jovanovich, 1992.

Good, Kenneth. *Into the Heart: One Man's Pursuit of Love and Knowledge Among the Yanomami*. New York: Longman, 1996. First published 1991 by Simon and Schuster.

Lizot, Jacques. *Tales of the Yanomami: Daily Life in the Venezuelan Forest*. Cambridge, UK: Canto/Cambridge University Press, 1991. First published 1976 by Seuil.

Perkins, John. *The World Is As You Dream It: Shamanic Teachings from the Amazon and Andes*. Rochester, VT: Destiny Books, 1994.

Steinvorth-Goetz, Inga. *Uriji Jami! Life and Belief of the Forest Waika in the Upper Orinono*. Caracas, Venezuela: Association Cultural Humboldt, 1969.